GUIDEI

MW01114311

Mission

Reaching the World

Una Jones, John Edward Nuessle, and Jodi Cataldo
Graphics by Jodi Cataldo
General Board of Global Ministries

MISSION

Copyright © 2012 by Cokesbury

This book is printed on acid-free paper.

ISBN 978-1-426-73641-4

Some paragraph numbers for and language in the Book of Discipline *may have changed in the 2012 revision, which was published after these Guidelines were printed. We regret any inconvenience.*

Contents

Called to a Ministry of Faithfulness and Vitality

Y ou are so important to the life of the Christian church! You have consented to join with other people of faith who, through the millennia, have sustained the church by extending God's love to others. You have been called and have committed your unique passions, gifts, and abilities to a position of leadership. This Guideline will help you understand the basic elements of that ministry within your own church and within The United Methodist Church.

Leadership in Vital Ministry

Each person is called to ministry by virtue of his or her baptism, and that ministry takes place in all aspects of daily life, both in and outside of the church. Your leadership role requires that you will be a faithful participant in the **mission of the church**, which is to partner with God to **make disciples of Jesus Christ for the transformation of the world**. You will not only engage in your area of ministry, but will also work to empower others to be in ministry as well. The vitality of your church, and the Church as a whole, depends upon the faith, abilities, and actions of all who work together for the glory of God.

Clearly then, as a pastoral leader or leader among the laity, your ministry is not just a "job," but a spiritual endeavor. You are a spiritual leader now, and others will look to you for spiritual leadership. What does this mean?

All persons who follow Jesus are called to grow spiritually through the practice of various Christian habits (or "means of grace") such as prayer, Bible study, private and corporate worship, acts of service, Christian conferencing, and so on. Jesus taught his disciples practices of spiritual growth and leadership that you will model as you guide others. As members of the congregation grow through the means of grace, they will assume their own role in ministry and help others in the same way. This is the cycle of disciple making.

The Church's Vision

While there is one mission—to make disciples of Jesus Christ—the portrait of a successful mission will differ from one congregation to the next. One of your roles is to listen deeply for the guidance and call of God in your own context. In your church, neighborhood, or greater community, what are the greatest needs? How is God calling your congregation to be in a ministry of service and witness where they are? What does vital ministry look like in the life of your congregation and its neighbors? What are the characteristics, traits, and actions that identify a person as a faithful disciple in your context?

This portrait, or vision, is formed when you and the other leaders discern together how your gifts from God come together to fulfill the will of God.

Assessing Your Efforts

We are generally good at deciding what to do, but we sometimes skip the more important first question of what we want to accomplish. Knowing your task (the mission of disciple making) and knowing what results you want (the vision of your church) are the first two steps in a vital ministry. The third step is in knowing how you will assess or measure the results of what you do and who you are (and become) because of what you do. Those measures relate directly to mission and vision, and they are more than just numbers.

One of your leadership tasks will be to take a hard look, with your team, at all the things your ministry area does or plans to do. No doubt they are good and worthy activities; the question is, *"Do these activities and experiences lead people into a mature relationship with God and a life of deeper discipleship?"* That is the business of the church, and the church needs to do what only the church can do. You may need to eliminate or alter some of what you do if it does not measure up to the standard of faithful disciple making. It will be up to your ministry team to establish the specific standards against which you compare all that you do and hope to do. (This Guideline includes further help in establishing goals, strategies, and measures for this area of ministry.)

The Mission of The United Methodist Church

Each local church is unique, yet it is a part of a *connection,* a living organism of the body of Christ. Being a connectional Church means in part that all United Methodist churches are interrelated through the structure and organization of districts, conferences, and jurisdictions in the larger "family" of the denomination. *The Book of Discipline of The United Methodist Church* describes, among other things, the ministry of all United Methodist Christians, the essence of servant ministry and leadership, how to organize and accomplish that ministry, and how our connectional structure works (see especially ¶¶126–138).

Our Church extends way beyond your doorstep; it is a global Church with both local and international presence. You are not alone. The resources of the entire denomination are intended to assist you in ministry. With this help and the partnership of God and one another, the mission continues. You are an integral part of God's church and God's plan!

(For help in addition to this Guideline and the *Book of Discipline*, see "Resources" at the end of your Guideline, www.umc.org, and the other websites listed on the inside back cover.)

You Are the Mission Connection
How Are You Elected and Connected?

You are not just a name on a list of church workers and volunteers, but a vital member of our church's connection in God's mission to the world. Thousands of United Methodists like you have accepted the challenge to support God's mission enthusiastically with your prayers, concern, time, financial gifts, and service. Your commitment to inspire and excite people about God's mission includes creating awareness and educating others about mission outreach in their congregations and communities.

This community of mission leaders includes a variety of individuals—women and men, young and old, people from different races and countries—bound together by our common goal to spread the good news of Jesus Christ and to minister to others in that name. Ours is a community of different kinds of congregations—rural, suburban, urban, large, medium, and small—with many perspectives on the world at large, but each congregation is an avenue through which God enters the world with power and grace to seek and save all people.

Depending on how your congregation is organized, you may be the chairperson of global ministries, the coordinator of mission, or the coordinator of outreach ministries. The coordinator of global ministries, mission, or outreach ministries (as well as other coordinators and chairpersons and other program leaders in local churches) is nominated by the committee on nominations and leadership development and elected by the charge or church conference each year. This body may limit the number of consecutive years a person may serve in one office, if it so desires.

It will be helpful if you are a member of the church council and the charge conference by virtue of this office so that you might most effectively report and discuss your programs for the congregation. In your work you are accountable to these bodies, and you work with the guidance of their chairperson and your pastor.

What Is Your Ministry?

As chairperson of the global ministries committee or coordinator of mission in your congregation, you are a vital mission connection between a needy world and your local church. Your role is to help educate your congregation members about the work of The United Methodist Church in God's mission and to provide opportunities for those members to respond through prayer and the stewardship of their time, talents, and resources. You can do this by providing mission opportunities and a greater awareness of both global and local mission through **mission education, mission experiences, and mission support**.

Jesus explicitly told us "the Way" to approach this: each person must love and treat others as he or she would want to be treated (Matthew 22:35-40). Jesus modeled how to be in *ministry with* one another, including widows, orphans, "the little children" (Luke 18:15-17), prisoners, the homeless, the outcast, the foreigner, the sick and disabled, the debtor, the oppressed, the occupying soldier—and even our enemies (see Matthew 5:43-47)—*but especially* society's most marginalized, "the least of these" (Matthew 25:45), with whom Jesus equated himself. (Matthew 25:35-40) Jesus showed us that *ministry with* means *being with,* being a caring presence, being in loving relationship with, standing with, standing in the shoes of, being in solidarity with, listening to, learning from, caring about, and respectfully responding to others as we would have them respond to us (see 1 Thessalonians 2:8 on sharing our lives; Romans 12:9-21). For more information about what it means to be in mission with others, visit www.ministrywith.org.

How Do You Make Connections for Mission?

One of your most direct connections for mission is through the General Board of Global Ministries, which connects the church in mission, equipping and transforming people and places for God's mission around the world.

MISSION AND EVANGELISM

The purpose of Mission and Evangelism is to coordinate and provide programs that enhance collaborative and responsive relationships with our global partners within The United Methodist Church and the world by sharing financial, programmatic, and personnel resources. The Mission and Evangelism program area of Global Ministries houses Mission Relationships, Justice and Discipleship, Missionary Services, and Mission Theology and Strategic Planning.

Mission Relationships identifies, develops, and nurtures respectful and effective relationships with mission partners throughout the world. Here you will find regional team offices for Africa, Latin America and the Caribbean, Asia/Pacific, and Europe/Middle East/North Africa as well as the Office of Mission Education.

Justice and Discipleship trains and develops leaders, communities and congregations for mission related to justice, freedom, peace, health, and wholeness. Justice and Discipleship connects ministries and networks with emphases on children, young people, women, the marginalized, and communities of color within the church and around the globe. In these offices you will find Congregational Development and African Diaspora, Hispanic/Latino Ministries, Asian American/Pacific Islander Ministries, Native American and Indigenous Ministries, Urban and Rural Ministries, Community Developers, Church and Community Workers, Human Rights and Social Justice, Scholarships and Leadership Development, Youth and Young Adults, Women and Children's Ministries, Special Program on Substance Abuse and Related Violence (SPSARV), Asian American National Plan, Hispanic/Latino National Plan, Korean American National Plan, and Pacific Islanders National Plan.

Missionary Services assists people who are responding to God's call to mission service as full-time missionaries or short-term volunteers. Missionary Services walks with these people through their discernment process; identifying, nurturing, and equipping volunteers and missionary applicants with the tools they need to explore serving as full-time commissioned missionaries, shorter term individual volunteers or on a United Methodist Volunteer-in-Mission team. The office also supports the missionary community through wellness, benefits services, and advocacy as missionaries retire or complete their service.

MISSION COMMUNICATIONS
Mission Communications works to educate and inform the church about mission. This program area includes New World Outlook magazine, Web, and social media.

THE ADVANCE AND DEVELOPMENT
The Advance for Christ and His Church (The Advance) is the accountable, designated mission-giving arm of The United Methodist Church that ensures 100 percent of each gift is used for its intended mission or ministry. The Advance develops mission partnerships and connects churches to missionaries through Covenant Relationships.

UNITED METHODIST COMMITTEE ON RELIEF (UMCOR)
UMCOR is the humanitarian relief and development agency of The United Methodist Church. UMCOR responds to natural and human-made disasters, particularly when the community is not able to recover on its own. UMCOR's administration is funded by the "One Great Hour of Sharing" offering. Therefore, 100 percent of gifts for humanitarian and disaster relief go toward such relief efforts.

One very important connection not to overlook is your own conference board of global ministries. Your chairperson and/or conference staff person for Global Ministries are invaluable resources to you as you seek to connect in mission.

Preparing Your Congregation for the Journey

Mapping the Journey—The Need for a Theology of Mission

One of the most important things you can do as the coordinator of mission for your congregation is to lay the foundation for all that you do in mission through mission education. Before you move forward in your journey into God's mission, help your congregation understand the "why"—the theology of mission.

The life of the Church of Jesus Christ is not to be a mere human organization, but a divinely empowered instrument of God's grace. St. Francis of Assisi is said to have sung: "Lord, make me an instrument of thy Peace", which is followed by his well-known graceful prayer of self-giving love. We will miss the power and the life-giving purpose of Christian faith if we limit our arena of concern and knowledge to only those persons we live among or meet along our journey. We are called as Christians to love the whole world for which Christ died and was raised to new life.

Grace is found in the body and blood of Christ, given in love for the whole world, all at once. To comprehend the fullness of John 3:16-17 we must grasp the truth that the most important persons are those whom we do not know and will likely never meet. Christ died and was raised to new life for all just as much as for ourselves and those we know and live among. This is grace upon grace, freely available to all. This is the foundation of and moving cause of Christian mission.

The global ministries of the church are the processes and methods by which we attempt to be with God in mission among all peoples and in all places at all times. To limit our field of ministry to a particular congregation or any geographic or thematic entity is to miss the limitless power of divinity that is incarnate in the world. Literally, we need to see the world through eyes of faith, observing all that God offers us in every time and place. We must live the truth of John 3:16-17—living for the whole world. As John Wesley said, "the whole world is our parish," meaning our area of concern and involvement.

For the Church to fully become God's instrument of grace in the world, whether locally, regionally, nationally, or internationally, we each need to understand and to state clearly our theology of mission, that is, what we believe about the world and God's mission in the world as the purpose of the Church.

By our activities in mission we become the signposts of the coming reign of God. The Church in mission is always pointing toward what God has done and continues to do in the world, by leading persons to participate in this grace-filled life. To engage in God's mission is to connect the Church as faithful witnesses to the reign of God that is constantly breaking into the world.

Our United Methodist understanding of mission is expressed in Our Theological Task in the *Book of Discipline*. As the Theological Task states: "Wesley believed that the living core of the Christian faith was revealed in Scripture, illumined by tradition, vivified in personal experience, and confirmed by reason." Thus we find Scripture, tradition, experience, and reason the sources of theology in the Wesleyan understanding, as the framework for doing theology.

In practice we then integrate these with the Four Goals of Mission of the Global Ministries, which then together express our United Methodist methodology for engaging in God's mission.

Identifying Your Destination—The Four Goals of Mission

The Four Goals of Mission, formulated by the directors of Global Ministries in recent years, express the mission responsibilities of the church as set forth in the *Book of Discipline*. Each of these goals is implemented through specific program strategies and is carried out in cooperation with annual conferences and other mission partners across the global connection.

The Four Goals of Mission of Global Ministries are:
1. **Make Disciples of Jesus Christ:** We will witness by word and deed among those who haven't heard or heeded the gospel of Jesus Christ. We will initiate, facilitate, and support the creation and development of communities of faith that seek, welcome, and gather persons into the body of Christ and challenge them to Christian discipleship. Where direct proclamation is not permitted, a caring presence becomes the means of Christian witness.
2. **Strengthen, Develop, and Renew Christian Congregations and Communities:** We will work mutually with mission partners in common growth and development of spiritual life, worship, witness, and service.

3. **Alleviate Human Suffering:** We will help to initiate, strengthen, and support ministries to the spiritual, physical, emotional, and social needs of people.
4. **Seek Justice, Freedom, and Peace:** We will participate with people oppressed by unjust economic, political, and social systems in programs that seek to build just, free, and peaceful societies.

The United Methodist Four Areas of Ministry Focus

To complete this analysis of your mission theology, it is important to integrate our denomination's areas of ministry focus. These four areas are another set of lenses through which we can focus the gospel work of making disciples of Jesus Christ for the transformation of the world. By focusing our common work in these ways we will enhance our efforts on behalf of God's mission in partnership with our Christian sisters and brothers around the world.

These areas of ministry focus are:
- developing principled Christian leaders for the church and the world
- creating new places for new people by starting new congregations and renewing existing ones
- engaging in ministry with the poor
- stamping out killer diseases by improving health globally

Your first step is to offer insights and biblical analysis for each of these areas to your congregation, seeking to place them within the mission theology work in which you have already engaged. How do these areas assist in advancing your ongoing vision for making disciples and becoming more globally connected from your community to communities of God's people the world over? What are the biblical principles that you identify within each of these areas?

Next, use these lenses to view the planning of your year-round program of mission education and mission involvement with and for your congregation. These next steps are described in the following chapters.

Specifically designed to resource congregations around ministry with the poor, Global Ministries created the With* campaign. With* provides resources for learning, mobilizing, connecting, and engaging with ministries and people to eradicate poverty. The With* website is an interactive and connectional space to share news, stories, best-practices, and a range of historical, educational, and multimedia resources regarding poverty and Ministry with the Poor. Go to www.ministrywith.org for details.

Your Congregation's Journey into God's Mission

Where Do You Begin?

Churches of every size can and should have interest, involvement, and partnership in God's mission. All it takes to begin is one enthusiastic person in the position of work area chairperson. A journey of a thousand miles begins with one step forward and that is where you might be right now. Start with your own mission awareness and interest, and then move your congregation to step out into God's world.

We hope these Guidelines help along the mission journey of a lifetime. No one need do everything suggested here, but everyone will find some practical, helpful, and useful ideas to be considered in planning a mission program for the local church. All of these ideas have been tested and used in a wide variety of churches—in churches of all sizes, locations, and levels of involvement. Decide where you are and take that step.

Provide Mission Opportunities for Your Congregation

1. Develop a continuous, year-round program of **mission education** so that the congregation will be better informed, more knowledgeable, and more motivated to be supportive of the mission outreach of the church.

2. Identify the needs of your community, your country, and your world and engage your congregation in **mission experiences** that seek to address these needs.

3. Seek to expand and increase your congregation's **mission support** and ensure that your congregation is provided every opportunity to participate financially in God's mission through the church.

Develop an Annual Mission Calendar

This year-round plan for mission provides guidelines and reminders of the connectional mission responsibilities to God's mission. These suggestions could support new opportunities to expand your church mission outreach.

January
• Launch or renew a Covenant Relationship with a Global Ministries missionary (see page 17 for details).

- Promote Human Relations Sunday—the first of six churchwide Special Sundays that The United Methodist Church asks all congregations to observe. It is acknowledged on the Sunday closest to the birthday of Dr. Martin Luther King Jr., who created better relationships among all people. Invite community developers (people who work on behalf of the church in local communities) or United Methodist service agencies to address the congregation. Go to www.umcgiving.org for details.
- Remind the church school superintendent to order the Children's Fund for Christian Mission materials from the General Board of Discipleship: www.gbod.org.

February
- Celebrate Black History Month.
- Begin to promote mission studies and United Methodist Schools of Christian Mission for adults, children, and youth. Go to www.unitedmethodistwomen.org/studies for details.
- Plan a mission volunteer experience. Consult your conference or jurisdiction Volunteer-In-Mission coordinators, or search this website for volunteer opportunities: umcmission.org.

March
- Promote One Great Hour of Sharing (second Special Sunday offering), essential to funding the United Methodist Committee on Relief (UMCOR). A gift to this offering underwrites UMCOR administrative costs, helping keep its promise that 100 percent of every gift you make to a specific UMCOR project can be spent on that project, not on home-office costs. Distribute materials and invite speakers who work with UMCOR projects related to hunger, refugees, and disaster relief. Go to www.umcor.org for more details.
- Make first-quarter contact with your missionary; send Easter cards. Use the Prayer Calendar, available from the Mission Resource Center at www.missionresourcecenter.org to find names and addresses of additional missionaries, deaconesses, home missioners, and Global Ministries' staff.
- Plan an Ubuntu Day of Service for the summer (August) in your local community using the Ubuntu Day of Service Kit at www.ministrywith.org.

April
- While celebrating Holy Week, Easter, or any Special Sunday, incorporate Global Praise music. Go to umcmission.org/resources or order from Cokesbury at www.cokesbury.com. Global Praise songbooks have songs of faith from diverse traditions around the world. The songs also affirm the global Christian faith of God's people.

- Celebrate Native American Sunday (third Special Sunday offering). Your offering nurtures outreach with Native Americans of all ages and provides scholarships for United Methodist Native American seminarians. Go to www.umcgiving.org for details.

May
- Celebrate Mission Month (Aldersgate Day) and recognize your local, national, and international mission involvement. Hold a Mission Rally Sunday—gather for a mission dinner or invite a mission speaker to address the congregation.
- Plan a Global Ministries mission seminar at the Global Ministries offices at the Interchurch Center in New York City or an interactive educational seminar in New York City with the United Methodist Seminar Program on National and International Affairs. Go to www.unitedmethodistwomen.org/programs, email info@umcmission.org, or call 1-800-UMC-GBGM.
- Celebrate Heritage Sunday. Heritage Sunday (May 24 or the Sunday preceding) is a Special Sunday celebrated by United Methodist congregations to reflect on our heritage, to celebrate the church's history, and look forward to the future. Go to www.umcmission.org/give for details.

June
- In preparation for vacation Bible school (VBS), visit a local mission project and design a field trip for the VBS.
- Encourage members to visit mission institutions or community centers during their summer vacation trips across the United States and around the world. Go to www.unitedmethodistwomen.org/give/missionmap for an interactive map of these locations.
- Engage in a mission volunteer experience planned in February.
- Celebrate Peace with Justice Sunday. (Note: The fourth Special Sunday offering is always the Sunday after Pentecost.) Global outreach through the General Board of Church and Society and annual conference-related peace with justice ministries transform lives. Go to www.umcgiving.org for details.

July
- Encourage church members to attend a School of Christian Mission. Go to www.unitedmethodistwomen.org/learn to find one near you.
- Sign up to receive UMCOR Hotline updates to stay connected with needs around the world: www.umcor.org.
- Use With* Campaign resources to organize a Bible study on mission and specifically Ministry with the Poor, one of the four focus areas of The United Methodist Church. The With* website, www.ministrywith.org,

provides resources for learning, mobilizing, connecting, and engaging with ministries and people to eradicate poverty.

August
- Hold the Ubuntu Day of Service you planned in March.
- Request updates on the needs and recommendations of the local mission projects you support in order to plan for next year.
- Renew subscriptions for the church's mission magazines or subscribe for the first time to stay current on the latest mission news and find program ideas:
  - ○ New World Outlook
    www.newworldoutlook.org
  - ○ Response
    www.unitedmethodistwomen.org

September
- Have a Mission Celebration. Set aside a weekend to train your church's mission committee and others interested in being involved in mission. Design the Sunday worship service to be focused on mission work. Invite itinerant missionaries and leaders of local community ministries to share. Establish new connections with missionaries, pastors, leaders, and churches in your community and across the world. On Saturday, offer a mission-focused task that the whole church can be involved in (i.e., packing first-aid kits, disaster buckets, meals, etc.). Offer a call and provide information for mission service.
- Plan mission programs and activities for the following year and submit an article to the local newspaper and/or news website to invite your community to be part of God's mission.
- Sign up for *connectNmission e-newsletters*: umcmission.org/resources.
- Plan a mission activity for the children and youth in your congregation. Go to www.gbod.org for ideas and resources.

October
- Promote World Communion Sunday (fifth Special Sunday). Invite people of different nationalities to participate in worship, dress the altar to represent different cultures of the world, serve communion with bread from different parts of the world, and incorporate more than one language into the litany. This offering supports scholarships for students preparing for Christian leadership in the world. Go to www.umcgiving.org for details.
- Participate in 10-Fold, an online interactive global gathering that puts faith into action. Go to www.10-fold.org for details.
- Plan a Children's Sabbath celebration for your congregation. Go to www.childrensdefense.org for information and resources to plan your event.

November

- In celebration of Thanksgiving create thanksgiving opportunities for your congregation to enhance ecumenical and interfaith relationships.
- Provide a mission education opportunity focused on supporting mission through The Advance. The program can educate the congregation about the function of The Advance in supporting mission with 100 percent of contributions and highlight specific Advance mission projects. Go to www.umcmission.org/give for resources on The Advance.
- Celebrate United Methodist Student Day (sixth Special Sunday). United Methodist Student Sunday, the last Sunday in November, funds scholarships and loans, supporting students who are finding new ways to serve God in the world. Go to www.umcgiving.org for details.

December

- Honor World AIDS Day (December 1). This observance helps to raise awareness and understanding of this deadly disease. Go to www.umcmission.org/resources for worship resources and educational materials to plan your observance.
- For Christmas, give a gift that changes the world. Make a gift to a specific project through The Advance, www.umcmission.org/give.

Connect Five Activities

1. *Covenant Relationship with a Missionary*

Since 1974, the **Covenant Relationship** program has enabled United Methodist congregations to partner with Global Ministries missionaries through prayer, financial support, and active engagement with missionaries in their ministries.

A Covenant Relationship is more than a financial commitment. Churches can send teams to work with missionaries, receive periodic updates on their ministries, and even communicate with missionaries in worship services or other events live via the Internet.

However, financial support is an essential part of a Covenant Relationship and enables Global Ministries to continue sending missionaries around the world. Financial support for United Methodist missionaries includes more than just salary support. It is the total resources needed to support a missionary financially, including health insurance, pension, housing, travel, training, and other expenses.

More than $7 million must be raised annually for missionary support through The Advance in order for Global Ministries to continue funding and sending missionaries around the world.

Through The Advance, 100 percent of your gift will go to missionary support. Your financial gift will support the entire missionary community in the name of one missionary.

Churches are asked to give at least $2,500 annually to support a missionary in a Covenant Relationship. However, churches that are able to should consider a larger financial commitment, enabling a missionary to reach their support needs with fewer Covenants and work more intimately with those congregations.

Churches, individuals, and groups can also give financial support to a missionary without establishing a Covenant Relationship.

How to Establish a Covenant Relationship:
- Establish a Financial Goal:
  - Congregations: $2,500 annual minimum or $5 per average church attendance annually.
- Contact your conference or district secretary of global ministries or The Advance office to obtain information about missionaries who are related to your annual conference. Also see the missionary biographies on the Global Ministries website: umcmission.org.
- Complete the Covenant Relationship form, which can be downloaded at umcmission.org/give. Return to: The Advance, 475 Riverside Drive, Room 350, New York, NY 10115; Phone: 212-870-3718; Fax: 212-870-3775; email: covenant@umcmission.org. Your church is encouraged to make a three-year commitment.
- Send financial support to your conference treasurer or to Advance GCFA. Please clearly designate the missionary's Advance number. Mail to: Advance GCFA, PO Box 9068, GPO, New York, NY 10087-9068.
- Consider the missionary as an extension of your church staff by listing him or her in your church bulletin, and prayerfully support the work of God's mission throughout the world.

2. Mission Moments
Have a member of the congregation give a short (four- to five-minute) presentation about some aspect of God's mission. **"Mission Moments"** might be used during the Sunday worship time, church school sessions, at church council meetings, or at any gathering of the congregation. They might be a set up as a dialogue or question-and-answer presentation with two or more people participating.

The content may address where money has been sent, what missionaries are doing, current issues and concerns, upcoming mission events, or pressing financial needs. Information for Mission Moments may be found in missionary letters, the Prayer Calendar, the Global Ministries website, or *New World Outlook* and *response* magazines. A presentation to the full congregation, even once a month, will do much to educate your congregation about mission and might be the most important activity you carry out in your position.

Mission Moments might also be highlighted in the monthly church newsletter, e-newsletter, or website and shared with district and conference newsletters, e-newsletters, or websites.

3. *Mission Displays, Bulletin Boards/Inserts and Social Media*
Use maps, posters, pictures, and brochures to make eye-catching **mission displays.** These are visual reminders that the congregation reaches out and is in mission with the world. Plan to change the display periodically, perhaps once every month or two.

Display pictures of Global Ministries missionaries, especially when you have a Covenant Relationship with a missionary. Include pictures of missionaries' projects where they are serving. Also include their current newsletter or website reports.

Bulletin inserts can relate to activities on your annual mission calendar. Go to umcmission.org or umcmission.org/resources for the latest bulletin inserts.

In all mission displays, mission announcements and other communications with your congregation be sure to lift up the ways The United Methodist Church is connected to mission through **social media**. You, your church, and individual congregation members can follow the latest mission news as it happens through social media. Provide links to Global Ministries Facebook, Twitter, and YouTube pages (see list below). If your church has its own Facebook page, Twitter account, or YouTube channel, use the "share," "like," or "follow" buttons to link to the mission stories and resources you find through Global Ministries' social media:
  • www.facebook.com/GlobalMinistries
  • www.twitter.com/connectnmission
  • www.youtube.com/ConnectnMission

4. *Mission Celebration Events (MCE)*
Through **Mission Celebration Events** a church has the opportunity to inspire, challenge, and train its members for missions, and connect them

with mission projects locally, nationally, and internationally. Through plenary speakers, workshops, music, and personal connection with missionaries around the world, churches can get actively involved with the global mission of the church. These events can be tailored to churches of any size.

Global Ministries can offer guidance on how to organize this event, as well as provide connections with missionaries, projects, and churches around the world. Send an email to missioncelebrationevents@umcmission.org.

5. *Volunteers In Mission*
Mission experience could include:

    a. Mission educational trips organized to visit mission projects/ministries in the local area, across the United States, and also globally. These trips provide a personal connection with the mission projects/ministries visited.

    b. Mission Volunteer experiences are opportunities to be involved in mission by doing hands-on mission work. Go to umcmission.org for a list of volunteer opportunities.

    c. UMCOR Sager Brown Depot work trips are opportunities for volunteers to provide support for disaster areas affected by weather or war. Volunteers work in the Sager Brown Depot in Louisiana assembling disaster-relief kits. Go to umcor.org or director@sagerbrown.org for details. UMCOR West (Utah Depot) work trips are available for individuals and groups to provide support for disaster areas affected by weather or war. Volunteers work in the UMCOR West Depot in Salt Lake City, Utah, assembling disaster-relief kits and working with local mission projects. Go to umcor.org or umcor@umcor.org for details.

    d. Plan a Global Ministries mission seminar at the Global Ministries offices at the Interchurch Center in New York City to develop a better understanding of the church in mission. Email info@gbgm-umc.org for details on a mission seminar. Plan an interactive educational seminar in New York City with the United Methodist Seminar Program on National and International Affairs to dig deeper into mission or a specific social issue. Go to www.unitedmethodistwomen.org/learn/seminars for details on the United Methodist Seminar Program.

Support for God's Mission

Prayer Support for God's Mission

prayer support for God's mission is absolutely essential for every congregation's mission program. Without the ongoing and fervent prayers of faithful church members, the mission program will simply be another charity to which they contribute. Your mission program must be understood as the vital link between your congregation and God's coming kingdom. As your congregation becomes spiritually involved in mission, miracles of mission education and support will occur.

The best way to promote the prayer support from your congregation is to encourage church members to obtain a copy of the annual **Prayer Calendar**: www.missionresourcecenter.org. This comprehensive calendar lists each of our missionaries and his or her birthday in addition to mission projects in the United States and around the world.

Lift up United Methodist mission projects during Sunday morning prayer times, as well as on a mission bulletin board and in the church newsletter. You might consider organizing a special Mission Prayer Fellowship of people committed to daily prayer for God's mission.

Mission Dollars and Sense!

How we handle the money we have is perhaps the most difficult issue for contemporary American Christians. Engaging in faithful stewardship of our financial resources can be the most freeing and liberating experience of Christian discipleship. Jesus' instructions to the disciples as he sent them off in mission were not to take any extra resources for the journey. God will provide.

How? "For laborers deserve their food. Whatever town or village you enter, find out who in it is worthy, and stay there until you leave" (Matthew 10:10-11). In other words, through mission giving, workers in the vineyard of the Lord are cared for by God through the faithful response of those of us who provide for their needs. Making the financial resources that God has given you available for those actively engaged in programs of God's mission is, in itself, also mission.

It makes sense that how we use our dollars and cents is how God is working in mission through us. We have significant financial resources in this nation, which God is calling us to use in mission, both around the world and within the communities in need in our country. Mission giving is mission.

The Biblical Guide to Mission Giving

The apostle Paul has given us a set of guiding principles by which we can organize such a faithful life of mission stewardship. He wrote to the church in Philippi concerning their generous financial support of his mission and ministry (Philippians 4:10-20), and in so doing gives us a rich commentary on how to faithfully support God's mission with our financial giving. Paul provides instructions for mission support through four principles for giving:

- First, and perhaps most important, mission support is a voluntary response to the gospel call, a spiritual investment in God's mission with faith that God will provide. "Not that I seek the gift, but I seek the profit that accumulates to your account. . . . And my God will fully satisfy every need of yours according to his riches in glory in Christ Jesus" (4:17, 19).
- Second, mission support is an expression of the community of believers as a whole, and individual gifts should contribute to the needs and focus of their church community (4:10). Christianity is defined and strengthened by its communal nature, and mission giving should reflect this strength.
- Third, mission support should be faithfully consistent, not just an occasional outburst of emotional awareness (4:15-16), for as Paul commends the Philippian church: "No church shared with me in the matter of giving and receiving, except you alone. For even when I was in Thessalonica, you sent me help for my needs more than once." Just as God cares for our needs daily, regularly, no matter what our needs are, so also must our mission giving be regular, no matter what the perceived need.
- Fourth, mission support should be channeled through responsible agents, not sent directly (4:18), for Paul received gifts from an acknowledged agent, noting the accountability in the process. Administrative accountability through a responsible agency ensures that everyone, givers and recipients, has a clear understanding of the use of the funds. This does not mean that the givers always direct their use, but a fully disclosed allocation unites giver and receiver in the common mission.

Mission giving is not so much about where your funds go or to whom they are given, but is your faithful response to God's call in your life to be engaged in God's mission. It is our spiritual investment that connects our lives with the lives of all who share in the gospel work of proclaiming the reality of God's ultimate reign, as we pray together, "Your kingdom come. Your will be done, on earth as it is in heaven" (Matthew 6:10).

Stewardship in God's Mission

Encouraging personal commitment to and support of God's mission is a crucial task of the chairperson of global ministries or coordinator of mission and your committee. Your work in this area is to seek to expand the mission giving of your congregation and prayerful support for all who are working in God's mission, at home and around the world.

Some churches focus all of their support on a specific ministry or specific region of the world while others give to various types of ministries throughout the world. Your committee should decide what model will best excite your congregation for mission.

- Every congregation is financially involved in mission through the variety of giving channels available to United Methodists. Since the mission committee helps develop a benevolence program for your church, it is important for you to be well acquainted with giving opportunities available to your church through The Advance (umcmission.org/give). You should encourage planned, systematic financial participation by the congregation in your chosen mission programs.
- Learn what your church members are already doing in local and global outreach and help them align that involvement with your committee's overall mission plans.
- The committee on global ministries or mission committee must study and plan with care to make the recommended budget a challenge to the giving potential of the congregation.

Developing Your Mission Budget

1. Your Mission Education Budget

The mission chairperson will also need to present to the church council budget recommendations for carrying out the program of mission education in the local church. This might include items such as costs for speakers on mission, national visitors, film rentals, School of Christian Mission promotion, leadership training, mission literature and supplies, postage, and other miscellaneous expenses. These funds are an integral part of our mission work since they allow you to share the good news of God's mission in your congregation.

2. Your Benevolence Budget

When the committee on global ministries or mission committee begins to make its plans for the benevolence budget, it must take into account the need of the world to receive and the need of the congregation to be involved in giving. It is good to ask: What does God expect of us? What is our opportunity as a community of Christians to further God's mission through our participation? When questions like these have been discussed, the matter of objectives can then be considered.

The church's potential is the next matter for the work area to consider. Questions such as these can be asked:

- In terms of financial ability, what could our congregation do in benevolence sharing if it really got serious about this matter?
- What could our members contribute?
- How much has our congregation participated in each cause this year?
- What is our total participation now?
- What is our per capita giving?
- What has been the trend in benevolence participation in our congregation during the past 10 years?
- Has benevolence participation kept pace with the growth of the congregation and with inflationary trends?
- Where do we want our congregation to be in its benevolence participation five years from now?
- What could we be giving and receiving eight and 10 years from now?

How Much Money for Mission?

These questions lead to another matter. The church council should discuss the question of what percentage of the total budget should go for benevolences. The common range in most congregations is 20–25 percent. However, many churches are working on the principle of "as much for others as for ourselves," or a 50–50 division.

If the church council accepts this as a goal, benevolences would include:

- World Service and conference benevolences/apportionments
- Advance Specials
- Special Sundays, such as One Great Hour of Sharing, Human Relations Day, and World Communion Sunday
- Youth Service Fund, the United Methodist Children's Fund for Christian Mission, and World Service Special Gifts
- Funds contributed through United Methodist Women and United Methodist Men that go for work outside the local church
- All other local benevolence causes.

When the committee on global ministries or mission committee has proposed a long-range objective for the church's benevolence program, the next step is to decide how far the congregation can go in that direction this year, and by gradually increasing the amount and proportion of the benevolence budget year-by-year, the goal can be reached.

The work area with a long view, a definite goal, and a plan for leading the congregation into the attainment of that goal year-by-year will enjoy the satisfaction of growing spiritually as participation in God's mission grows in your congregation.

The Advance

Your committee on global ministries has a particular interest in The Advance program of mission support and will want to work hard to promote this. The Advance is a mission program begun by our church in 1948. Since that time, more than $1 billion has been given by United Methodists to support God's mission in the United States and around the world through "second-mile" giving.

These dollars enable us to advance the cause of Christ through planting new churches, training new pastors, supporting missionaries, building sustainable economic development, providing scholarships and medical assistance to women and children, and hundreds of other programs like these.

- Advance projects are supported by voluntary and designated gifts from individuals, churches, groups, estates, and annual conferences.
- Advance projects are in nearly 100 countries around the world, including the United States.
- Advance projects are chosen by those most directly affected and based on the priorities of the local people. Local episcopal leaders and planning groups determine the priority of projects in their region then submit proposals requesting these projects be approved as Advance projects.
- If projects are approved, they receive an individual Advance number.
- Local churches and individuals can give to any approved project and 100 percent of their gift will reach the designated project. Advance gifts are tracked and monitored to ensure accountability and transparency in the use of your gifts.
- All missionaries also have Advance numbers, used by donors to give to their financial support. Missionary support is a top priority for The Advance.
- Conference Advance projects are approved and administered by your annual conference board of global ministries, conference council on ministries, and annual conference office.

Planning Your Advance Program of Mission Giving

First, be sure the congregation will be able to pay its World Service commitment before considering The Advance as a means of giving to mission.

World Service is "first-mile" giving funded by your church's annual apportionment giving. The Advance program is "second-mile" giving and depends on World Service funds in order to maintain its 100-percent gift promise.

Next, consider supporting a missionary through The Advance (see Covenant Relationships, page 17). Many of our missionaries work at Advance projects and need support for both their missionary funding and project. Contact your district or conference secretary of global ministries for projects your conference or district has a commitment or special interest. There also might be places of particular need related to and promoted by your district and annual conference. If you have questions on specific projects or programs go to umcmission.org/give.

Finally, find ways to obtain support for the Advance projects or missionaries your committee selects: through the church budget, special offerings at events or mission Sundays, or fund-raising by church classes or groups. When these gifts have been gathered, they should be sent with a clear designation of their intended use, using the project number found in the Advance Giving Resource Guide or umcmission.org/give.

Giving Online
umcmission.org/give

Giving Through Your United Methodist Church
Make your check payable to your local church. Write the name of the ministry and the Advance code number on the check. Drop your gift in any United Methodist church offering plate or give your gift to your church treasurer so that your church and annual conference can credit your gift.

Give by Mail
Make your check payable to ADVANCE GCFA. Write the name of the ministry and the Advance code number on the check. Send your check to:

Advance GCFA
P.O. Box 9068, GPO
New York, NY 10087-9068

Give by Phone
Credit card gifts can be accepted by phone. Please call: (888) 252-6174.

Missionary Support

Missionary support is vital to the life and future of The United Methodist Church. You can support a missionary through the Covenant Relationship Program (see page 17) with individual gifts or estate planning. Learn more at umcmission.org/give.

Other Thoughts on Mission Giving

There are many independent groups and nondenominational churches, sects, and others, both effective and ineffective, which appeal for funds from United Methodist congregations and individuals. Members need to understand that they have many relationships and commitments as a congregation in partnership with the whole Church throughout the world. In many of these relationships, funding comes only from our church members, so churches in many parts of the world are depending upon us as United Methodists.

Your congregation's committee on global ministries or mission committee can help members be aware of all the church is doing to support mission and can explain the importance of giving through our own United Methodist connection.

We have a dependable system for assuring the safe delivery and distribution of gifts through The Advance because of our worldwide network of churches. Contributions do not go through outside agencies but through accountable Christian congregations and church organizations. This is a story that needs to be shared with your congregation.

Participating in God's Mission
Your "Response-Abilities"

as both believers and actors in God's mission, you are called to organize and plan your responsibilities, or "response-abilities" using your God-given abilities to respond to God's call to be sent into the world, which God so loves (John 3:16). The lifelong journey of responding to all of God's mission is a call to organize your congregation with:

YOUR PRESENCE
You bring leadership to God's mission through your active presence in the life of the church, in all arenas of church activity: lifting up the needs of God's mission in worship, decision making, program planning, and implementation.

YOUR PRAYER
You bring spirituality to God's mission as you actively engage in prayer for missionaries and partners in mission throughout the United States and around the world, reminding others in the church to pray for these persons. Connecting your prayer lives with those of God's people around your nation and other nations will broaden your faith vision and deepen your spiritual presence.

YOUR PURSE
You bring the resource of your purse to God's mission, as you intentionally decide on the use of the financial resources God has provided you with for the advancement of this mission. A local church with a mission vision will have a budget that reflects all these areas of mission. Where and how you choose to use the income and accumulated wealth of your congregation will proclaim to the world your understanding of yourselves as either global citizens of faith, or a locally limited religious club.

You live out your missional perspective of God's world through your presence, your prayers, and your purse, all offered to the glory of God.

Keeping Your Eyes on the Destination
As you integrate your "response-abilities" in making disciples of Jesus Christ for the transformation of the world, always keep your eyes on the destination. The prophet Isaiah provides a powerful reminder of God's vision for the coming kingdom—the ultimate destination:

> For I am about to create new heavens
> and a new earth;

the former things shall not be remembered
  or come to mind.
But be glad and rejoice forever
  in what I am creating;
  for I am about to create Jerusalem as a joy,
    and its people as a delight. (Isaiah 65:17-18)

The global new heavens and new earth are created out of all the local "Jerusalems"—including your local church—in Wesley's words, "to sing psalms, and pray, and hear the Scriptures expounded." From there we go forth into global ministries that heal, feed, nurture, care for, and empower the people of the whole world for new life.

These, then, are your tasks and responsibilities as a chairperson of global ministries (or mission) and committee on global ministries (or mission) in your local church. It is hoped that this Guideline will help you know where to begin and how to go about your important functions in the life of your congregation. Take that first step on your mission journey of a lifetime and be a partner in God's mission with thousands of coworkers throughout the Church.

Make Your Plans Carefully
Carry Them Out Prayerfully

Evaluating Your Mission Program

You, your team, and your church want to have a vital ministry. Periodic evaluation with established measures allow you to avoid the twin dangers of (1) continuous doing without evaluating and (2) evaluating simply by way of numbers. One way to guard against the "we've always done it that way" syndrome is to build into plans when and how you will evaluate and the measures by which you will judge your efforts.

The evaluation process brings together your vision and mission for your church's overall mission program, the goals and strategies used to bring that vision to fruition, and the measures by which you compare your results with your desired outcomes. Measures are indicators of activity and impact.

The example below shows one way you might evaluate your mission program. In this case, the example provides a definition and outcome (based on ideas laid out in the chapter, "Your Congregation's Journey into Mission," page 13, and other guidelines laid out in this book). The example also supplies a few possible strategies and measures to evaluate your mission program. Using both qualitative and quantitative measures, you can see the impact of your mission program on members of the congregation. After evaluation you might adjust your program to better meet the interests and needs of the community.

SAMPLE: EVALUATION OF MISSION PROGRAM

Mission Education	Mission Experiences	Mission Support
Definitions: Develop a continuous, year-round mission program that helps congregation be better informed and more knowledgeable about the church's role in mission.	Engage your congregation in hands-on service opportunities that seek to address the needs identified by your community, your country, and your world.	Expand and increase your congregation's mission giving and ensure that your congregation is provided every opportunity to participate financially in God's mission through the church.
Results: Persons are more motivated to be supportive of the mission outreach of the church.	Persons volunteer for mission service projects to work with their local and global community.	Persons participate in mission giving to support mission in the local church, nationally, and globally.
Strategies: 1. Train mission team on theology of mission 2. Use With* campaign resources to lead Bible study on ministry with the poor.	1. Plan an annual mission experience (either in the U.S. or globally) 2. Host missionary or speaker from local mission program to share their experience in mission.	1. Celebrate six Special Sundays in worship and Sunday school 2. Educate congregation on giving opportunities through The Advance (with bulletin inserts, speakers, newsletter updates, etc.)
Measures: 1. 30% of congregation participates in Bible study; 75% of participants demonstrate understanding and practice the United Methodist theology of mission 2. 50% of Sunday school teachers emphasizing mission in their classes.	1. All participants in mission experience report greater understanding of mission and mission opportunities 2. 50% of participants in mission experience commit to future mission work with the church 3. 30% of congregation participate in missionary speaker event	1. 50% of congregation gives to Special Sundays 2. 50% of congregation gives to mission through The Advance. 3. One family or group in the church (e.g., Sunday school class, youth group) supports a missionary through the Covenant Relationship program

Resources

to assist you in planning your congregation's journey into God's mission, the denomination produces numerous resources. This booklet is one of them, and it is one unit in a larger series: *Guidelines for Leading Your Congregation: 2013–2016*. Other booklets in the series that you might find helpful are *Church Council* and *Small Group Ministries*. These are available from Cokesbury: *www.cokesbury.com*.

Global Ministries Resources

"connectNmission" (Global Ministries e-newsletter)
umcmission.org

Global Ministries (mission study books, brochures, maps, and other resources)
www.cokesbury.com
umcmission.org/resources
phone: 1-800-672-1789
email: customerservice@umpublishing.org

Global Praise (music resources)
umcmission.org/resources

New World Outlook (magazine)
newworldoutlook.org

response (magazine)
www.unitedmethodistwomen.org

10-Fold (online interactive global gathering that puts faith into action)
www.10-fold.org

United Methodist Women (resources and mission studies)
www.missionresourcecenter.org
phone: 1-800-305-9857
email: cs@missionresources.org

With* (campaign to raise awareness, educate, and inspire people around ministry with the poor)
www.ministrywith.org

www.facebook.com/GlobalMinistries

**umcmission.org

www.twitter.com/connectnmission

www.youtube.com/ConnectnMission